Habits of Losin

Text copyright ©

legal Disclaimer

The information contained in this book and its contents is not designed to alter or take any form of medical or professional advice; And not to replace the need for independent medical, financial, legal or other professional advice or services, as may be necessary. The contents and information in this book have been provided for educational and entertainment purposes only. The material and information contained in this book is compiled from sources deemed reliable, and is most true to the knowledge, information and belief of the author. However, the author cannot guarantee its accuracy and validity and cannot be held liable for any errors and / or omissions. In addition, changes are made to this book from time to time as needed. Where appropriate and / or necessary, you should consult a professional (including but not limited to your physician, attorney, financial advisor or other such professional advisor) before using any of the suggested remedies, techniques, or information in this book .

Table of Contents

Introduction

Changing your habits is one of the most effective ways to lose weight. And each person has different habits in life. However, in this chapter, I am going to show you some habits that you should change. If you want to change a healthy person alive, control your weight and feel better.

If you do a Google search on the word "habit" then you will find thousands and thousands of articles on that subject. But unfortunately, those articles do not meet expectations when someone tries to implement it. Therefore, in this e-book, I am going to talk about the habits that are scientifically proven to reduce weight.

Miraculous methods do not exist and are not effective, they can endanger your health, especially those that do not carry a label in their presentation.

By maintaining healthy habits you can establish a lifestyle and diet which is undoubtedly the best way to lose weight. The important thing is to become aware and understand that the term diet leads to a set of healthy eating habits that should not be limited to a certain amount of time.

When you make a goal of losing weight, it is important to change your habits which are beneficial for your body; And nutrition is one of the fundamental pillars of health and well-being.

If you want to lose weight, then without "bounce" you should consider a change in habits to achieve a healthy lifestyle. Unlike so-called "miracle products", achieving healthy habits does not involve risk to your health.

Therefore, in this e-book, I will introduce the 7-mini habits, simple everyday habits to keep fit and healthy, habits that persist for a long time with ease in gradual weight loss, actions that science has Effectively set out to get the figure you've always wanted. And healthily.

Remember that if the weight increases in a given period of time, it will also take time to reduce. Do not despair; The key is to achieve a healthy lifestyle that includes perseverance, attitude and attachment to one's goals. Yes! You can do this!

let's enjoy!

Habit # 1: Reduce intake of fried, junk and creamy foods

It is normal for us to enjoy junk food from time to time; This is the fastest option for those who have a very busy and stressful life. Therefore, many people depend on this food as a major part of the daily diet. However, it is not recommended as it is harmful for health.[i].

The baking technique of frying and junk food involves the complete immersion of food in a hot lipid medium (fat or oil), so that the final product has a higher amount of fat than the food from which it starts, especially if the technique is in Not done correctly. Therefore, the fried products are high energy density. Changes in the nutritional value of the product, however, depend on a number of factors: the quality and nature of the raw material from which it is divided, the presence or absence of the batter, dissolved or cooked, the number of oils used and the time it takes to reenter. : Has been used, or the condition of temperature and cooking time.

In addition, certain substances harmful to health are produced during processing, such as acrylamide or products derived from oxidation and thermal degradation of fats.

In this regard, it has been pointed out that consuming those foods in moderation can be part of a healthy and balanced diet. The problem is that while they are usually made in medium and low-quality oils, they are eaten very often (as fast and pre-cooked food) and are a vehicle for calories, fat, and salt.

Effect on health, weight and body fat

The excess of fried foods favors overweight and heart deformity. For their contribution of fat, they contribute to increase the percentage of cholesterol, triglycerides and body fat.

The high energy density of these products means that frequent consumption of them is related to more imbalanced eating and heavy weight (overweight or obesity), excess body fat and certain types of cancer (breast, stomach and prostate) There is a high risk of developing. other).

In addition, the presence of unwanted substances derived from fried foods increases the risk of suffering from some pathologies, such as cancer and heart diseases, so it should be ensured that the technique applied reduces the production of toxic compounds. And it is true to limit its consumption to a sporadic frequency.

Decoglue for frying correctly

If you do not want to get away from fried foods completely, what should you keep in mind for cooking? Nutritionists provide the following recommendations:

1. Respect the time and temperature stated by the manufacturer for frying or cooking potatoes, crickets or dumplings. Do not let them get too dark. Therefore, cook them to a reasonable degree. It is advised not to go above 160–180 inC in the oven and above 160–175 inC in the fryer or frying pan.

2. Use olive oil for cooking, even for the fryer, "because it has a boiling point higher than sunflower and allows frying at

lower temperatures. It also keeps more chips and frying Generates less waste than it is. It is convenient for you to remove it. Small pieces, pieces or pieces of food that break apart during frying. In this regard, it is preferable if it is virgin olive or extra virgin. High oleic sunflower is also a healthy option.

3. Apart from oil, fried foods should be of quality.

4. Abusive reuse of frying oil is not recommended, so you should discard those that have been used on many occasions. There is no consensus on the maximum number of oils as the oil can be reused as it depends on many factors (one type of food, how fried...). Neither the old should be mixed with the new oil nor, preferably, would it be destined for the same type of product.

5. Avoid eating too many toasted or crispy foods.

6. Soak the potatoes before cooking. If it is in boiling water, they have to be sieved for a minute or two; If the water is hot, then 20 minutes is enough; And if it is in cold water, with one hour. In this way, the starch separates and the water remains cloudy. Rinse them before drying and baking. Acrylamide is formed when starch is caramelized. Starch is soaked in water by soaking potatoes, so there are fewer raw materials to make acrylamide.

7. To prevent oil from overheating, do not overfill the fryer or pan. In this way, you will also achieve that food absorbs less oil. If you prepare a lesser amount of packaged ration, then adjust the amount of time as well.

8. You keep the fat (oil) abundantly in a deep container (frying pan or fryer) and wait until it is fully heated, so that the food does not get steamy before it completely

submerges. In this way, the obtained heating is homogeneous and a quick surface crust is created that prevents excessive absorption of fat while providing a crunchy sensation when cutting and the softest texture inside.

9. A correct frying should be done in a short period of cooking, as the lipid content of the final product will remain in contact with the oil longer and higher production of harmful substances will be avoided.

10. Put the fried product on absorbent paper before serving to remove excess oil, as there is an increased risk of fat entering the interior during cooling.

What should you do?

- **Start by switching to healthy ways**
You should focus on preparing a list of what should be eaten during the week to include fresh products and healthy ingredients.

- **Avoid shopping when you need to feed**
Generally, when you are hungry you feel hungry due to food which you are saving from ending up in the stomach.

- **Look for the best variety in foods that are beneficial**
Your body should adjust to the healthy choices that you are going to consume; Your goal is to avoid junk food, fried foods, breaded, seasoned or creamy.

- **Do not exaggerate**

Do not reduce calories drastically; Go a little bit, try to avoid eating junk food for two days, then three days until it disappears.

Habit # 2: Walk for at least four days per week, 1 hour

Walking is one of the best "tricks" to lose weight. It improves many aspects of your physical and mental health. Now, is the best time to get accustomed to this practice. In this chapter, search for the walk that suits you best.

several studies[ii]Show that for those who do little or no exercise, walking well twice a week can be a source of health. The biggest advantage of walking is that no prior training is required and it is accessible to most people.

Benefits of walking for health

There is not one explanation for this benefit, but several:

You activate your metabolism: Namely, the speed at which the body uses the energy derived from food. At each step you take, hundreds of muscles burn those calories and stop them in such a way that they become obese.

Improve your muscles: When you walk at a good pace, insulin secretion decreases and other hormones that increase exercise by converting fatty acids into energy in your body. The result is that you lose fat, but you gain muscle and your figure becomes smoother and more molded.

Improvement of intestinal infections: Vibration occurs in your body when walking in favor of movements of the small intestine, which helps to speed up the rate of emptying and dealing with constipation. At the same time, you reduce abdominal bloating and eliminate toxins.

Increase your self-esteem: Apart from physical improvement, regular practice of sports brings significant emotional benefits. When you exercise, you release endorphins (a hormone that is associated with a feeling of pleasure). This enhances your well-being, which will help you to remain stable with exercise and to have more self-control during meals or breakfast between meals.

Three types of walking according to your body shape

How much should you walk? To reap the benefits of walking, I propose a progressive scheme with three types of walking, which increases its difficulty. Follow it and you will see how your health and your figure will improve.

1. Basic Walk for Beginners

In order to see its effect, you must walk for one hour a day. This is the time when your metabolism needs to start "burning" fat.

How to choose the route: Take advantage of a known journey from your city or town, but remember that you must go at a constant speed and non-stop to look through the shop windows. In total, you have to do 4 km in 1 hour. So you will burn at least 230 kcal, although the higher your weight, the more energy you consume.

Start little by little: Heat the first 5 minutes, walk 50 minutes faster, and devote the last 5 to cooling. Your goal should be to improve a bit less and not to move farther or faster than any other.

2. Rapid but controlled walking

If you are already accustomed to doing some physical exercise, then you can adopt this type of walk. To do this, you only have to speed up some sections of the route.

Proposed route: Once familiar with the basic technique of walking, it is time to incorporate a few minutes of intense practice into your route which will help you spend even more energy. Take small steps more often and you will gain more speed. You can also choose to climb a hill and burn 40% more energy. In total, you will have to travel 6 km in 1 hour.

How to do it: Start with a 5 minute warm-up, do 35 more runs at a brisk pace, increase the speed for the next 15 minutes and finally, spend 5 minutes cooling down.

3. Combined treadmill for fast weight loss

It is proven that, if you change your rhythm while exercising, you burn fat faster. Once you have attained a better physical shape, I suggest that you take a soft turn in your walk.

Recommended Program: Its purpose is to travel 7 km in an hour on a route that allows you to walk and run at the same time. Apart from burning more calories, running can help prevent monotony during travel. You will also define your silhouette as you will participate in many more muscle operations.

Program a trip well: Look for possible places where there is a pause to rest at the right time.

How to do it right: After 5 minutes of warm-up, very brisk walking or 10 more minutes, stopping for another 5 minutes, increasing speed by 15 more minutes, exercising toning for one more time, speeding up again for 15 minutes And finally cooling.

It is important to stop and perform squats such as toning or stretching exercises to stretch the leg muscles.

Best time of day to walk

The best hours of the day are the first hours of the morning to hang out and the last hours of the afternoon (7 to 10 pm), especially if it is hot.

Doing it at the beginning of the day helps you start the day with energy whereas doing it in the late afternoon can help you eliminate stress and get better sleep.

Lose more than sticks: "nordic march"

This modernity arose in the 1930s from the hands of skiers, who were able to train in summer and autumn. It was supposed to run with the help of ski-like sticks.

In 1997, a Nordic and a Finn developed special cans that anyone could use to popularize the practice, which they named "Nordic Walking".

What should you do?

- **Walk with flexibility**
Flexible shoes will help you, but you should still try to move comfortably, one after the other, allowing for a natural and flexible movement of the feet.

- **Don't take big steps**
If you do this, you decorate the feet and ankles. It is better to take small steps according to the size of the person.

- **Keep good posture**
This will allow you to breathe well and maintain the bodyline. Chin up parallel to the ground and eyes about 3 meters in front.

- **Arms should not be calm**

The arms should be in motion, stationary, like the front and back pendulum.

- **drink water**

Drinking water before and after exercise is important to maintain your hydration. If you manage to walk for more than two hours, drink isotonic drinks for athletes.

- **Rest one to two days a week**

This is very important so that your body can be repaired and muscles reorganized. If you cannot lose a day of exercise, try another type once or twice a week.

- **Do not continue walking if you feel pain in your chest, or you are feeling tired or dizzy**

If you have trouble breathing or cannot interact with anyone while walking, stop and consult your doctor immediately.

Habit # 3: Eat slowly

There are many people who eat fast and carelessly. But the reality is that eating slowly is considered a wise approach that benefits us many. One of them is losing weight[iii].

Eating well and in small amounts is also good for the cardiovascular system because it prevents or limits weight, which is one of the risk factors for cardiovascular diseases.[iv].

It may take some time to slowly accept the habit of eating, but you will get this when you start seeing results in your weight.

It is proven that fasting is not good for your weight or your health: you become bloated, digestion is more expensive and your BMI increases, among other things.

To eat slowly and consciously, it is very important that when you sit at the table you pay attention to the environment and the way you act.

How does it affect the environment in which you eat

Location and company at the time of eating effects, and more. With these simple gestures you will create a conducive environment to enjoy the task of feeding yourself:

1. Create a pleasant atmosphere

It is important that it is comfortable and quiet. A comfortable environment where you can sit down to eat (you should avoid eating while sitting on the couch) that invites you to consciously focus and enjoy your meal.

2. adequate lighting

To illuminate the dining room, it is recommended to use lamps that light soft tones which allow to create a comfortable atmosphere. Two useful options are floor lamps and ceiling lamps with an overhead light which also saves space.

3. Put on relaxing music

Soft and slow ambient music will also help you relax during your meal as it helps to create a good environment without being a distraction.

4. Turn off radio and TV

You will avoid getting distracted. Reading newspapers, reviewing work notes, browsing tablets ... and above all, moving mobiles away from the table: breaking food rhythms, changing the peace, and interrupting conversations are also not convenient for you.

5. Prepare the table with care

Arrange the table practically, but it allows you to get away from the crowds and worries. To do this, keep a nice tablecloth, simple cutlery and crockery that fit. It is also very stimulating to place a vase with fresh flowers, even some candles that warm the environment.

6. Watch the presentation

Food should be a pleasure in all aspects. Therefore, even if you do not consider yourself a chef, try to prepare in an attractive and colorful way to delight yourself with the eating process.

7. Reminder that helps you

Place a clock on the table. Watch the time and give yourself at least 30 minutes. The key is that all meals last for that time.

How to eat with less worry

You will think that sitting at the table worrying or feeling hungry, you will eat very fast. These tips will help you do it calmly:

1-sit down to enjoy the meal

This happens rapidly and unknowingly by standing and eating. Relax to enjoy the meal and sit watching the posture. Keep the feet flat and parallel and align the columns. Relax the stomach and keep it throughout the meal.

Use 2-forks and knives

Throw them between bites, placing them next to the plate. This simple gesture will help you enjoy the food more, as you can focus more on the mouth, giving you an account of the joy that you bite into what you eat.

Take 3 small bites

Prepare the dish with food in large portions, but then cut it with a knife and fork. Make it into small pieces and chew each bite at least 20 times. The sooner you finish in small amounts, the sooner you will be satisfied.

4-Serve in a small bowl instead of a plate

In a smaller bowl, less volume will fit and you will eat less. So, you will not go to serve yourself a large quantity of food. If it is pasta, it is good to use this technique because it will be full without adding a large amount of pasta to the bowl.
5-Smell and observe what you are going to get

Analyze its color and its appearance. Tell yourself what you think, describe it. And enjoy its aroma too. Not only will you eat more consciously, but your brain will "start" before you even start eating.

"Listen" to your stomach

Do you really notice hunger, the feeling of emptiness? Or do you notice that cravings for food are more concentrated in your mouth than in your stomach? Distinguishing between one thing or the other will help you eat without haste.

Pay attention in the kitchen

Remember that your way of cooking is also important and affects the way your body processes food.

Choose Whole Foods. Opt for raw vegetables and other fiber-rich products and dispersion with very soft preparations. Add nuts, croutons or whole grains to soups and yogurt.

Pasta or rice; When its texture is "firm", they chew you. Also, your glycemic index is low, and you benefit from it.

A trick for a slow move

1. Practice with a grapefruit... right at the beginning of the meal. Try this exercise:
2. Paying attention to the breath and breath you are giving, take three deep breaths and relax.
3. With the help of all your senses (sight, smell, taste, and touch) take a grain of grapes and enjoy it.
4. Move it inside the mouth before cutting it gently.

What do you get from this exercise?

When eaten consciously, its purpose is not only to nourish the body, but also that food is a pleasant experience for the mind and senses.

If you have noticed that you eat fast and want to enjoy the benefits of eating slowly, then there are some tips to achieve this. read on!

What should you do?

Chew each bite thoroughly. Try to see the taste of each ingredient of the dish. This will keep your attention focused on what you eat and delay your intake.

- **Drink water between bites**

This is important because it helps prevent intake and slow down food.

- **Leave the cutlery behind each bite on the plate**

After one bite, place the cutlery down on the plate to continue the intake. This trick will allow you to devote time to each bite that enters the mouth and, therefore, allows you to eat more slowly.

- **Use cutlery**

This technique can help you because with it you always eat more slowly if you feed the food with your hand to the mouth. For example: If you eat sandwiches without cutlery then you will fast with them.

- **Always eat at the table**

This way you can focus on the rhythm you eat and it will be easier to eat slowly, while if you stand or do any other task, you quickly finish without eating anything. Will give

- **Eat without being distracted**

This means that you should eat away from the workplace, computer, or TV, as they will catch your attention, allowing you to eat quickly without thinking.

- **Eat more fiber**

This is important because hard foods, with too much fiber, require more chewing and, therefore, delay the speed of intake.

Habit # 4: Reduce Alcohol Consumption on Special Occasions

Excess alcoholic beverages can be produced in your body and can cause many harm to health, moreover, you should also be aware that an abusive intake of alcohol can damage your physical appearance, ie you quickly gain fat. can do^v.

One of the worst enemies of the diet is alcohol, they have become an important part of human culture and there is a misconception that consuming alcohol in any social situation is more fun. The truth is that alcohol consumption has a very negative effect on any weight loss process.

Why stop drinking alcohol?

People who consume alcoholic beverages daily have 100 and 200 calories in their body.

- Improvement in senses (especially smell and taste)
- Reduce your chances of suffering from infectious diseases
- Contribute to a good mood

In addition, quitting alcohol reduces body odor, improves nail and hair health, and can help you lose weight.
Weight loss occurs due to this habit:

1. It makes food more

When you consume some alcohol, you are at risk of consuming junk food (especially snacks).

If instead, you drink mineral water or natural juice at lunch or dinner, you will distance yourself from the temptations of baking and prefer healthier options.

2. Hide Calories

Without realizing it, a cup increases calories significantly, even more than food.
For example, a "drink colada"[vi]"It has 160 calories, one daquiri, 170 calories, one wine 120 calories and one whiskey, 100 calories.

Although you may think that it is not too much, the problem is that you do not drink just one drink, but many, some recipes.

3. fix fat

Perhaps you have read or heard the phrase "alcohol store fat". This is completely true as it urges the body to produce more estrogen.

This hormone stimulates the accumulation of fat (especially in women).

4. Metabolism slows down

When you drink alcohol, the body does not have the ability to burn fat or digest properly.

Many hours after intake you still feel "heavy", regardless of how much food you have eaten.

5. It makes you tired

Drinking too much alcohol leads to dehydration, resulting in fatigue. You don't feel like doing anything except sleeping or lying on the couch and watching TV.

Don't forget: Without movement, there is no weight loss.

What should you do?

Be more aware of your alcohol consumption patterns and plan ahead. This can help you reduce your alcohol consumption. Record the amount you drink and set some goals. How to do this

- Keep track of how many drinks a week you have in your wallet or on your calendar or on your phone.
- Know how much alcohol is in a standard drink: a 12-ounce or bottle of beer (355 ml), a 5-ounce glass of wine (148 ml), a mixture of soda-containing wine, or 1 cocktail or drink of alcohol.

While you are drinking:

- Set the rhythm yourself. Do not drink more than one drink every hour. Drink water, soda or juice between drinks with alcohol.
- Eat something before drinking and in between drinks.

To control the amount you drink:

- Avoid people or places that don't want you, when you drink, or entice you to drink more than what you need.
- Plan other activities that do not involve drinking for days you are drinking.
- Keep alcohol out of your home.
- Make a plan to manage your desire to drink. Remind yourself why you don't want to drink or talk to someone you trust.
- Create a kind but firm way to refuse a drink when you are offering one.

Habit # 5: Keep a food record or diary

Self-control of our behavior favors weight loss, as indicated by a study published in Addictive Behavior, and one of the ways to achieve this is to keep a record of everything consumed or drunk, including the food diary It is said, as well as our usual recordings. Training[vii].

Keeping records of food and training facilitates the identification of harmful habits and their change for healthy people. With these records, you can see potential errors, advances and failures over time, but above all, you know what you eat and how much you move, being fundamental to losing weight.

This is because once you know what your habits are in terms of food and exercise, it is easy for you to identify the people you need to change and make them healthy. Self-assessment and the reinforcement that you achieve lets you see how you are changing and you are in favor of that change of habits and weight loss for your goals as well.

Be sensible

Obviously, the success of these food and exercise magazines depends largely on how honest you are at the time of filling them: perhaps the case of food is the most obvious because you should write everything down. Yes, the Coca-Cola that you have taken in the afternoon is also counted, and that piece of cake that you have been offered in the office in the mid-morning, even if it was very small. Often, you usually eat your head only what you eat inside the staple food, forgetting the rest and it can play against you.

Bollywood

You may have to modify your program to make changes in your diet and exercise. This may mean eating early or preparing your lunch to avoid fast food. Along with diet and exercise, you should make other lifestyle changes. Getting enough sleep can help you lose weight. Sleep affects hormones in your body. It contains hormones that tell your body whether you are hungry or full. You should also try to reduce your stress levels. Many people relate stress to weight gain.

Desire to think

When you start a weight loss plan, there are things to keep in mind. There can be an obstacle that makes it difficult for you to lose weight. Or which may cause weight gain at first. In return, you need to be careful where you get advice. Your weight loss plan should be safe and successful.

Obstacles

Most people who are trying to lose weight have one or more obstacles. You may have bad habits that started at an early age. Breaking habits is difficult, but it is possible to do so. Your doctor can help you make changes, one step at a time. But anyway, let's see what you can do.

What should you do?

You should include many information in your daily food diary. these:

- **How much?**

Expand the quantity of food / beverages. It can be measured in volume (half a cup), weight (2 ounces) or several ingredients (12 potato chips).

- **What kind?**

Write the type of food / drink. Be as specific as possible. Don't forget to write extras such as dressings, sauces or spices. For example, butter, ketchup or sugar.

- **When?**

Keep a record of the time of day you ate.

- **Where to?**

Pay attention to where you eat. If you are at home, write in which room; For example, on the dining table, in the kitchen or on the couch. If you are away or if you are in a car, write the name of the restaurant.

- **With whom?**

If you eat alone, write "alone". If you are with friends or family, list them.

*Activity:*In this column, describe all the activities you do while eating. It can work, watch TV or play games.

state of mind:You should also include how you feel when you dine. Are you happy, sad or bored? Your mood may be related to your eating habits and can help you change them.

While keeping food diary, there are some basic rules to keep in mind:

- **Note everything**

Keep your diary with you throughout the day. Write down everything you eat and drink, no matter how insignificant it may be. Whether it is candy, small soda, or a good meal, calories increase.

- **do it now**

Do not trust your memory at the end of the day. Record your customized food data throughout the day.

- **be specific**

Record your food how you eat it. If it is fried chicken strips, just do not write chicken. Be sure to include extras. It can be a sauce on your meat or a dressing on a salad.

- **Guess the amounts**

If you have a piece of cake, estimate the size (2 "x 1" x 2 "). If you have vegetables, record how much you ate (1/4 cup). When you eat meat , Then serve a 3-ounce ripe. Is about the size of a card.

Habit # 6: Drinking water before meals

As it is more a question of habit than anything else, we can think that in the end the nutrients of the ingestion dishes end up equally in the organism and, then, reduce the order of consumption.

However, it is the nutrients of each preparation that you ingest that can give importance to the order in which you eat.

Why is it beneficial to drink water before eating food?

We all know that drinking water is healthy and necessary for our body. However, sometimes it is our cost, especially if we are forced to drink without thirst.

However, your body needs to stay hydrated and so it is necessary, for example, to know that children and the elderly drink enough water to create adequate internal balance.

- Water helps you eliminate toxins
- Hydrates your organs
- Transports minerals to cells and allows to complete all metabolic processes
- Water has no calories and therefore, it does not make you fat
- Drinking water before meals controls your calorie intake.

According to studies, drinking a glass of water before meals helps us to become satiated and lose weight.[viii]. Stomach feels full and controls the feeling of curbing hunger that we consume more than calories.

It is important to note that drinking water before meals will not make you feel "bloated". It not only fills your stomach, but it also stimulates kidney function so that you can cleanse the body better.

Avoid cold water before meals

This is another fact that you should keep in mind. There are people who are accustomed to drinking cold water. It is more pleasant and comes in handy during summer time.

However, it is better to avoid it. The reasons are as follows:

- Cold water greatly increases the pH of the organism and decomposes it, causing some difficulty in digesting food, which makes gastric mission difficult.
- Cold water is highly recommended in those moments when you feel tired after exercising or after a great effort. It hydrates you quickly and lowers body temperature.

On the other hand, drinking water at room temperature and even warming up before a meal or simply waking up is very suitable for achieving all these aspects:

- It acts as a good diuretic and facilitates purification of toxins.
- Water at room temperature improves digestion and allows you to take care of your intestines, without causing them to suffer from the effects of too hot or too cold liquid. This is very suitable in case of irritable colon sufferer.
- Hot water protects you from infection and reduces the presence of viruses and bacteria.
- Hot water favors most enzymatic processes in the body. They are better processed and the intestines absorb nutrients better.

- This allows you to digest and purify the fat needed to lose weight.

What should you do?

- Always keep water on hand. Always try to have a bottle at work, a small bottle that is always in your purse and always a glass of water next to you at home. In this way, you overcome the laziness of going for water when you are thirsty.
- Drink a glass of water half an hour before each meal. If you make five meals a day, and this trick you drink at least five glasses of water.
- If you forget to drink water, set an alarm. Although it seems a lie; Some people always forgot to drink water, especially at work. So they set an alarm on the computer every hour.
- Lay a glass of water on your table as you lie.
- Drink a glass of water every morning as soon as you wake up. Drinking water in the morning will help you stay hydrated and will not cause headaches in the morning.
- If you have trouble drinking water, then take tea, green tea, chamomile, lemonade, Rooibos tea.[ix].
- set goals. For example, drink your half liter bottle of water before 12 noon. This can help motivate you.
- If you do not like the taste of water, then add lemon or juice to the water. For example, start with 50% water and 50% juice, and gradually increase the percentage of water.

Habit # 7: Eat a strong breakfast and light meals

Breakfast is the most important meal of the day, as it gives us the energy needed to start the day. We should avoid eating during dinner so that fat does not accumulate.

Losing weight means what you put in your mouth, and having more breakfast and light dinner has many benefits.

The saying goes: "Breakfast like a king, lunch like a prince and dinner like a beggar." Experts predict that energy and nutritional contributions should be divided into five intakes, as food supplements favor the body to absorb nutrients. What can you do to lose weight without going through strict diets or suppressing food? Analyze what you eat when it is sunset, that is, review your dinner.

What does dinner

Supper has to provide 30% of daily calories[x]. The current pace of life and lack of time breaks good eating habits, causing us to ignore or overeat this food. How is dinner related to weight loss?

You start with the premise that breakfast should be taken more prominently than dinner because it gives you the energy to start the day. The opposite happens with dinner, which represents a period of inactivity in which you rarely burn calories consumed.

Misconception

Many people have the misconception that dinner represents the strongest meal of the day when the reality is second. Dinner should be light and just in calories, it is not necessary to eliminate it completely. If you snack a little, you risk a lot of hunger after a few hours and end up longer than the next meal. An abundant dinner encourages you to store fat, and in turn, can affect the quality of sleep.

Under no circumstances should you make the mistake of skipping dinner, starving or restricting carbohydrates. It is enough that complex carbohydrates are potent and you avoid sugary-rich products.

Breakfast and dinner are both two staple foods that help you get nutrients and balance the diet. The idea is to eat everything, avoiding excess. If you focus on protein, then you should choose those that come from low-fat foods.

It all comes down to achieving a negative energy balance. In other words, spend more than you want to swallow.

What should you do?

- Dinner should be light and only in calories.
- At dinner, you should never eat full, as you have said that the excess will accumulate in the form of fat and affect the quality of sleep.
- It is wrong that you have to ban carbohydrates at dinner; You just have to know which ones to choose.
- At dinner, you should focus on proteins, which come from low-fat foods.
- Make a dinner that helps cleanse the body or that is easily digested.

Dinner is a staple food to lose weight. It has a lot of effect according to how we eat it. Eat as much light as possible, it is better for us if we want to lose weight. A clear example: If we eat large amounts and fall asleep, we sleep, all the energy and fat we eat to stay in reserve, and then we get fat.

The conclusion

During this e-book, we have looked at 7 mini habits that will help you lose weight. We have seen how to reduce the consumption of fried, junk food and creamy foods which is very important as it affects a large number of the world's population.

We have also seen that when you have a habit of walking from 15 minutes-1 h, at least four days a week which helps you to lose weight. Walking is one of the best "tricks" to lose weight. Eating slowly, chewing food properly is essential for good digestion and it helps you lose weight.

Reducing alcohol intake is also another habit. The truth is that alcohol consumption has a very negative effect on any weight loss process. Keep a food record or diary and training promotes weight loss by self-control of your behavior.

Drinking water before meals is a good habit for people with many benefits. Water helps you eliminate toxins, hydrates your organs, transmits minerals to cells and allows all metabolic processes to be completed. Even if you drink a lot of water, it does not make you fat because water does not contain calories.

Finally, we have seen the last habit of having a strong breakfast and a light dinner. Breakfast is the most important meal of the day, as it provides you with the energy needed to start the day. You should avoid overeating during dinner so that fat does not accumulate.

To conclude I recommend you to be positive as this is the most important part of this change in habits. Enjoy food, do it comfortably, with awareness of what you eat and without feeling guilty if one day you eat something that you know is not the right thing to do. You will not be served with remorse and guilt.

Negative thoughts can make you bad and feed you less than bad foods. Think that all the changes in your habits can only bring you good things.

The good thing is that all those habits are simple, practical and fun to learn, and have been proven by experts. Now you have everything in your hands if you really want to change your body without going through specific diet and exercise.

Printed in Great Britain
by Amazon

26356391R10030